The Reproach is Lifted
BARACK OBAMA PRESIDENCY

Dr. Tino W Smith

authorHOUSE®

AuthorHouse™
1663 Liberty Drive, Suite 200
Bloomington, IN 47403
www.authorhouse.com
Phone: 1-800-839-8640

First published by AuthorHouse 1/8/2009

ISBN: 978-1-4389-4439-5 (sc)

Printed in the United States of America
Bloomington, Indiana

This book is printed on acid-free paper.

Dedication

I would like to dedicate this book to all of the forerunners who paved the way for Senator Barack Obama to be elected the 44th President of the United States of America. We can never forget the efforts of Thomas Mundy Peterson, the first African American to vote in an election in 1870 or Vernon F. Dahmer, Sr., the civil rights activist who sacrificed his life so that African Americans could register to vote.

I also would like to dedicate this book to the residents of the state of Indiana and the city of Terre Haute who helped to turn one of the reddest states in the nation into a blue one for the first time since 1968.

Acknowledgements

I owe a great debt to LaKina Curry for her understanding and patience as this book developed and took some unexpected twists.

To my wife, Nicole, her wisdom and insight are a tremendous benefit.

I want to thank both Tino II and BreAnna for sacrificing their time with me to allow me to work on this project.

To my brother, Hugh Smith Jr., for his revelatory insight to things pertaining to the thoughts and subject of this book.

To my mother, Georgia Howard, for her continual support in every task I attempt to do, and her foresight even on this project.

Finally, to Barack and Michelle for allowing God to use you both as trailblazers and for being the vessels to lift my reproach.

Contents

Introduction

For the last seventeen years, the month of November and the date of the 4th has always been special to me. In 1991, I was elected as a Calhoun County Commissioner and in 1992, my daughter, Bre'Anna was born. My mother called her an election baby. Sixteen years later it was time to celebrate our daughter's sweet sixteenth birthday.

I pondered whether to give her a party so that her family and friends could be a part of the celebration, but instead I decided that we would go to Chicago, spend the whole day together, and perhaps be a part of history. Well, in keeping with the tradition of November 4th being so special to me, on my daughter's 16th birthday, Barack Obama was elected the 44th President of the United States of America. Alongside the many thousands of spectators and with tears flowing down my cheeks, I asked God, "What does this all mean?"

The Bible instructs us that *"with all thy getting, get an understanding"*. I needed to know. I have always felt that when something historical takes place --as in this election-- then something must also occur in the spiritual. My brother Hugh, while the Holy Spirit was speaking through him began to share with me that "the reproach has been lifted from the African American people".

I knew at that moment that my way of contributing to the healing that President-elect Obama mentioned in his victory speech in Chicago was to write the inspiring book "The Reproach is Lifted". Obama stated, *"This victory alone is not the change we seek. It is only the chance for us to make that change. And that cannot happen if we go back to the way things were. It can't happen without you, without a new spirit of service, a new spirit of sacrifice. So let us summon a new spirit of patriotism, of responsibility, where each of us resolves to pitch in and work harder and look after not only ourselves but each other."*

I told my mother when I phoned her from the plane that on this day "I've been born again". I'm an American and proud to be one. I had not stood and recited the pledge of allegiance since that cold Tuesday, on December 10, 1991 during our Calhoun County Board of Commissioners meeting in Marshall, Michigan when I stated, "No justice for all". Throughout my life, I have experienced time and time again that justice was not for all. This book however, is not intended to mention any of those past experiences.

The Apostle Paul said, *"forgetting those things which our behind and reaching forward to those things which are before"*. That is my promise to My President -- a new spirit of patriotism. I trust that this book will give meaning and understanding of what we now can do and become. *"To those who would tear the world down: We will defeat you. To those who seek peace and security: We support you. And to all those who have wondered if America's beacon still burns as bright: Tonight we proved once more that the true strength of our nation comes not from the might of our arms or the scale of our wealth, but from the enduring power of our ideals: democracy, liberty, opportunity and unyielding hope. That's the true genius of America:*

that America can change. Our union can be perfected. What we've already achieved gives us hope for what we can and must achieve tomorrow."

Those are words from our next president. The image of our first family, Michelle Obama, Sasha and Malia is remarkable. The state of Indiana, where I have lived for the past eighteen years, is a state with an ugly history of racism. Indiana changed and broke a 44-year curse. As Vice President-Elect Joe Biden said, "A Democratic president hasn't carried the Hoosier state since Lyndon Johnson in 1964.

Indiana turned from a red state to a blue state. That is not the victory. As President Obama stated, *"Americans sent a message to the world that we have never been just a collection of individuals or a collection of red states and blue states". We are, and always will be, the United States of America.* It is the seed that Dr. Martin Luther King Jr. planted in 1963 when he stated that one day they will not be judged by the color of their skin but by the content of their character. That dream came to fruition this year on one of my favorite days, November the fourth. My hope is this -- People do change! I give you "The REPROACH IS LIFTED".

Dr. Smith

Change We Can Believe In

One of the most remarkable things to come out Barack Obama's election is the restoration of hope among black men everywhere. There was what I would like to call a *sweet vindication* that took place on November 4, 2008.

Black men have been known for either their talents or their crimes, but on November 4, 2008, a black man was finally known for something else. Senator Barack Obama won 52% of the national vote. There were no hanging chad controversies and there were no recounts until the midnight hour. The United States of America had overwhelmingly sent a message to the rest of the world that it was indeed ready for a change.

Many people took offense when during the campaign; Michelle Obama made the comment that for the first time in her adult life she was proud of her country. Republicans jumped on the comment to try and show that she was "unpatriotic". Even Cindy McCain added her two cents by stating that she has always been proud of her country.

These individuals, especially an heiress to a 100 million dollar fortune, can never know what it is like to come out of your mother's womb already in second place or to be in a race with one hand tied behind your back – in other words—with the odds already stacked against you.

One can go to any part of this country and run into a black man who 1) was kicked out of school because educators didn't know how to reach him 2) unable to get a job because of the lack of proper training or 3) denied a job because of past convictions. When faced with these types of circumstances, some black men become bitter and stop seeking the "American" dream, while others become enraged and become a menace to society. All the counselors, psychologists and psychiatrists in the world had no answers for "growing up black".

<u>Reproach</u> *verb* **(1) To express disapproval of, criticism or, or a disappointment in (someone). 2) To bring shame upon; disgrace.** *Noun* **(3) blame; rebuke. (4) One that causes rebuke or blame (5) disgrace; shame.**

In this book, I will not mention names because the purpose of this book is to uplift and not attack. I am referring to all the conservative talk hosts, conservative black authors and organizational leaders. I believe that all of our beliefs, opinions or worldviews are based upon our personal experiences and realities.

When there is a reproach on a group of people, the ability to remove that reproach is not an easy task despite the best efforts of self-empowerment, building strong family units and spiritual black churches that help individuals to reach their full potential. Conversely, it is easy for one who has been under reproach to accept the teaching of hatred and animosity between the races.

Now I am not saying that the election of Barack Obama will erase the stench of the past hundreds of years. What I am saying is that it marks the beginning of a new way to look at us. This man from day one brought a message of HOPE and wherever he spoke the message was still the same – CHANGE WE CAN BELIEVE IN. Obama was speaking about a change in Washington D.C., and a different direction from the failed Bush years, but I saw the greater message of a change in perception. It is my objective in writing this book to not to repeat the same information that we have been taught for the past four hundred years regarding American history and race relations. I am even going to attempt to stay away from mentioning dates and other historical events that would only bore you. What this book will address however, is the new freedom that should be embraced by not just African Americans, but by the white Americans and all the other ethnic groups that helped to put the Honorable President-elect Barack Obama into the White House. This man is an authentic African American with a white Kansas-born mother and an African father who now sits as the Commander-in-Chief over the free world.

I, like Obama, have higher education degrees. I take care of my wife and my family. I am a good son, good brother and a good uncle. I own my own business and care for the flock that God has entrusted me with, and yet I can still tell you that I carried the rage inside of me. As I have mentioned before, I like many before me, have felt the wrath of racism and have the battle scars to prove it. There was a popular refrain several years ago that stated, "There is no JUSTICE, it is JUST US".

Because of this silent rage within me, I stopped reciting the Pledge of Allegiance years ago. As my children got older and became more involved in school activities and sports, my refusal to stand or acknowledge the flag was often times uncomfortable. I, however, never wavered in my conviction that until America changed her evil ways, I would not and could not recite the pledge.

On that beautiful November 4th evening, as I watched with millions of other fellow Americans the nation elect its first black president, my rage slowly began to dissipate and was replaced with pride and yes, for the first time, HONOR. I was finally proud to be an American. I believe that we are witnessing a true healing for our nation. Now I know that there are still some racist idiots out there that are absolutely fuming at the fact that Obama will be the 44th president of the United States. Just as Jesus said that the poor would be with us always, I firmly believe that the ignorant will be with us always as well. The majority of Americans however saw that during these perilous times, Obama is the man for such times.

Think about this – we (black men) have always thought to be of lower intelligence. Even in the arenas that we have had our greatest success – sports-- we were never thought to be the "smart quarterback" or the "smart point guard". Those were terms that were generally assigned to the physically-inferior white players. During these dire times, however, Americans are putting the hopes, dreams, aspirations of themselves and their children into the hands of a black man. This is true vindication indeed!!!

As I mentioned in my introduction, when a shift occurs in the natural, I believe that wholeheartedly a shift is occurring in the spiritual as well. When I speak of healing, I am talking about Americans of all races now being able to be better neighbors to each other. Hispanics, African Americans, Asians and whites now being able to truly fellowship is within our grasp if we allow it to be. It has often been said that when trials come, families should grow stronger and more resolute.

The collapse of our economy (the trial), caused the nation to shift what had been a trademark of the past eight years – cultural division. What the Bush/Cheney administration accomplished more than anything else during the past eight years was division in the country. Everything was about us vs. them, red states vs. blue states, immigration vs. hard-working Americans, small town "values" vs. big city corruption. Americans had tired of this division and in stepped a person who was ready for such a time as this. CHANGE WE CAN BELIEVE IN.

Many dismissed this populist tone as utopian nonsense and were absolutely shocked when masses of people began to turnout to hear about this message of change and hope. As I stated earlier, when the economy began to crash around us and people began losing their 401ks in addition to already losing their houses and everything else, they said enough is enough. When McCain tried to use the old Republican way of attacking Obama's character, all it did was hurt McCain. Why? Americans were ready for change.

This tells me that we no longer need to separate the races. Whites do not need to feel pressure that the owe blacks or other minority groups any form of special treatment due to their guilty of slavery. We are all part of the human race, which makes us family. The people of the United States of America were willing to set aside long ingrained beliefs of inferiority, racism and stereotypes because their suffering outweighed any other beliefs they may have felt. The fact that they felt that a black man was the best person to help ease their suffering is only fitting. I see it as America coming full circle and finally closing the chapter on what has been a very long book. CHANGE WE CAN BELIEVE IN.

Indiana Goes Blue

One of the most intriguing aspects of this past election was the role that Indiana played on the electoral map. Granted, we now know that Obama would have won the presidency without Indiana, but the fact that he won Indiana was very newsworthy.

Indiana had been a red state for the past forty-four years. The last Democratic president to get Indiana was Lyndon B. Johnson. As a matter of fact, Indiana had been one of the few states that on election nights would be instantly colored red as soon as the polls close. This year was different.

Who would win Indiana was still being debated even after Obama had been declared president. As soon as the polls closed, McCain was given the early edge but as the night wore on and the results began to matriculate in from Lake County it was becoming increasingly obvious that the tide had indeed turned. Why is this so significant? This is significant because of the history of Indiana.

Although Indiana is comfortably situated in between Illinois and Ohio, its politics and makeup can easily be aligned with the South. Indiana has a very ugly racist path with the KKK pretty much running state politics in the 1920s. It was in Indiana that one of the most disturbing and grotesque lynchings took place.

The southern part of the state is notorious for its racist undertones and takes great pride in its reputation.

It was in Indiana; however that Obama decided to open several field offices and sign up hundreds of volunteer to spread his message of Hope and Change We Can Believe In. Media reports that this was no easy task. During the primary run, several volunteers reported receiving threats and were racially taunted. Their attitude and determination, however, never wavered. Obama himself visited the state close to fifty times during the primary and presidential campaign. Hoosiers took notice. McCain, probably believing that he would never lose Indiana to a Democrat, much less a black Democrat, only visited the state twice.

Another item of particular interest to me was the role of Terre Haute in this whole affair. According to election data, for the last one hundred years, Vigo County voters' trends have predicted the national election. Karl Rove, President Bush's former campaign operative, even stated on CNN to watch what the Vigo County voters do.

Now for those of you who don't know, I have pastored in Terre Haute for over seventeen years and actually lived in Terre Haute for over ten years. Terre Haute, Indiana is about a hard luck town as it comes. Its reputation precedes itself. It was in Terre Haute that I achieved many things as a pastor, but it was also in Terre Haute that some of my most serious injustices took place as well.

In 1998, I pretty much dominated the headlines of the local paper, *Tribune Star*. The newspaper, along with county and local officials, conspired to shut down my residential group home. My name and my business were left in ruins. I had a local prosecutor making threats to prosecute me and fellow pastors writing letters to the editor against me. I don't think anyone would have blamed me if I had decided to throw in the towel against such insurmountable odds. I however, persevered and in ten years have not only been able to rally my church and community supporters, but also engage them in the political process to witness the election of the first African American president.

What role did Vigo County play in this national election? Well, if Vigo County is indeed the bell weather for national politics, then the rest of the nation definitely took its cue. Terre Haute, a town hit hard by high unemployment and poverty rates due to the closing of several factories, overwhelming voted for Barack Obama.

The rural areas held true to form and voted for McCain, but Obama won every large city in Indiana as well as the college towns of South Bend, West Lafayette and Bloomington. That a state with such a rotten racial history could vote for someone as different as Barack Obama is absolutely inspirational. To show you how ironic that is, the governor of Indiana, Republican Mitch Daniels, won re-election in a landslide. What that shows is that many Hoosiers crossed over when it came to picking their next president. Amazing! I am so proud of my adopted state and my adopted town of Terre Haute!

For the Sake of the Call

Now that the unthinkable has happened, African Americans must take heed not to blame President-elect Barack Obama for situations beyond his control. Granted, his message of change and hope resonated with millions of people worldwide, but we all know that change does not happen overnight.

Obama is aware of this as well and spoke of such on *60 Minutes* in his first televised interview after winning the election. Often times we become disappointed in our leaders, when circumstances in our personal lives do not change for the better. For many blacks, Obama's election was the turning of the tide. They saw his election as a chance to right what had been centuries of wrongs. To these individuals I say please give our new black President the chance to make it happen.

There are some in our community that because of their years of ingrained inferiority believe that things are now going to be WORSE now that Obama has been elected. I cannot help but call this form of thinking "the seasoning". For so long, many black Americans were conditioned to always sense the worse in ourselves. That is because of the four hundred years of mental abuse that was inflicted on the race. It is hard break loose from this type of thinking. Yes, there have been individuals who appear to have overcome the horrible part of our history in America.

They say that they feel no hatred or animosity. Again, I say, that it is not as easy as it sounds. This type of seasoning can even be seen in the Bible. Allow me to share with you an aspect of the story of Moses that has gone overlooked.

Moses was God's chosen leader for the children of Israel or the Hebrews. He was born during a time of great persecution of the children of Israel and the Bible stated that his people cried out for a "deliverer". This man Moses was born for such a time as this. His first recorded act as a man was harshly resolute, and prophetic of his future powers of deliverance. He saw an Egyptian beating up a Hebrew and Moses killed the tormentor. The next day he saw two fellow Hebrews fighting and endeavoring to restrain them, he tried to speak to the aggressor who in turned insulted him by bringing up the fact that Moses had killed an Egyptian a day earlier.

> *"And when he went out the second day, behold, two men*
> *of the Hebrews strove together; and he said to him that*
> *did the wrong, 'Wherefore smitest thou thy fellow?' And*
> *he said, 'Who made thee a prince and a judge over us?*
> *Intendest thou to kill me, as thou killed the Egyptian?' And*
> *Moses feared, and said, Surely this thing is known."*
> Exodus 2:13-14

This was the first of a long succession of insults that Moses was to receive from his countrymen; however, it did not stop Moses from doing what was God's purpose for his life – deliver his people.

I am certain that as sure as the sun rises and sets, Obama will face many insults as well. Some older black Americans, who lived through the civil rights movement, believe that Obama's presidency will just give racists even more ammunition to "keep the black man down". I have heard them say that we can now no longer claim racism when we are turned down for things because the president of our country is black. In so many words, we now become victims of reverse discrimination because our president is black. That, my friend, is the seasoning that I spoke of earlier, and that same very thing happened to Moses as well. Instead of rejoicing in their newfound freedom from slavery an inhumane treatment, the children of Israel blamed Moses for "bringing them into the wilderness to die!"

I can hear the seasoned blacks saying, "At least we were getting hired before, now we cannot get anything!" If we allow this type of thinking to permeate, then it will be divide and conquer all over again. Guess what? We will all be back at square one. We must not allow this to happen!

When the slaves were brought over from Africa, they had to be "seasoned". To make the slave fear the owners, torture and some times even death was used. Proud black African men and women were beaten, stripped naked and humiliated in front of their families. To escape such abuse, rewards were given to those slaves who reported acts of disobedience amongst fellow slaves. Some of these rewards were more food, less work or residence in the master's house. That is where the term "house Negro" or house slave was derived. This was the insult that was levied against President-elect Obama by Ayman Zawahiri, the 2nd commander of Al Qaida.

We must toss aside what can only be described as "stinkin' thinkin'" and rejoice in a victory that I believe was God-ordained. Trust me, God did not bring us this far to let us fail now. To my African American brothers and sisters, the reproach has been lifted by God Almighty.

The African slaves who provided most of the labor that built the White House never imagined that a black man would ever own the embossed stationery that reads 1600 Pennsylvania Avenue. Even the dreamer himself, Dr. Martin Luther King, Jr., might not have imagined that forty short years after his assassination, we would be planning an inauguration of the first man of African descent to ascend to the presidency. No minority of any ethnicity has ever looked beyond the scarce representation of a few Senators and seen anything that suggested that the door knob of the Oval Office could be opened by anything other than the hand of a middle-aged white male.

One of the youngest presidents in the history of our nation will bring new shades to the canvas of white leaders who came before his unprecedented political career. Senator Barack Obama has proved to be a biracial icon who can mobilize blacks and whites alike. Perhaps his mixed heritage gave him the multicultural background needed to be culturally bilingual, creating the dialogue that may bridge our divide.

As Barack Hussein Obama places his brown hand on that black Bible to take the oath, it will not make him merely the President of the blacks who admire him nor the leave him indebted to the whites who assisted him. He cannot acquiesce to the liberals who support him nor vilify the conservatives who do not. He must remain a philosophical centrist who garners our best and brightest from both sides of the aisle. He must transcend all of that and rise to the global perspective of his calling and through it serve his God, his country and the rainbow coalition of the people of this great nation. We can hope he can re-establish the international respect we have lost and gradually convince the watching, waiting world that a change for us is good for them.

It ignores the fact that many other blacks have run for president and walked away without winning a primary, much less the presidency. Neither Shirley Chisholm, Jesse Jackson, Al Sharpton nor Alan Keyes amassed black support the way Obama did.

Barack Obama and the "Moral" Issues

Allow me to address another issue that came up during the recent election. Many African American churchgoers were torn over Obama's positions on homosexuality and abortion. Members in my congregation and throughout my organization felt that as children of God, they just could not vote for Obama. I chose to vote for Obama because I thought that he was the most honest candidate in the dishonest and non-Christian system in which we operate. I realized that in spite of all our rhetoric, America is no longer a Christian nation. We are a secular democratic republic. We are **not** a theocracy – where the rule of God prevailed liked in ancient Israel.

Even by the time Jesus came, Israel was far different than it had been in the times of Judges, I and II Kings, and the era of the prophets. During Jesus' time, Israel was under the rule of the Roman Empire and the reign of the non Jewish evil King Herods. Surely, you would agree that our current society is far more similar to ancient Rome than to Ancient Israel. Every wicked thing that we see today was happening during the Roman Empire and to some extent during the rule of Herod. Nowhere in Jesus' teaching did he tell his followers to fight to legislate righteousness in the society or to end homosexuality or abortion through activism. In fact, Jesus said, *"My kingdom is not of this world!"*

Paul and the other New Testament writers lived under the tyranny of the Roman emperors. History tells us that the same issues that plague our current society – abortion, homosexuality, etc, were also prevalent during the time of the apostles; yet, in all of their preaching and in all of their writings no where do they encourage the early church to stand up against the empire and transform it through politics or legislation into a righteous nation. Conversely, in all of Jesus, Paul, and the other apostles' teaching, there is no condemnation of the secular society or its leadership. The severest condemnation was always for the religious people who had missed the entire point of the true meaning of the Kingdom of God.

If God intended the church to transform society through laws and politics, wouldn't he have mentioned that somewhere in his Holy Scripture? The early church turned their secular world upside down not through protest, the ballot, or political activism, but through spiritual revival! Has God's program changed in the 21st century?

I think that the focus of so many Christians on taking over our government by "force" is really a distraction. It keeps us from carrying on the real business of the church – coming into unity of the faith unto a perfect man, turning from our wicked ways, humbling ourselves to pray and seek his face. Christians want to legislate out homosexuality and immorality, when both are quietly allowed to run rampant in many so-called Christian churches. Is this the way to change the world?

With the exception of Israel, where the law had a specific purpose which was to serve as a school master bringing us to grace, God has always dealt in choices. In the garden of Eden, he allowed the choice between the tree of life and the tree of the knowledge of good and evil. In Jesus and Paul's time, there was the choice between good and evil, and so it is today. Is the kingdom of God to be ushered in through the people of God crushing out all other choices? I believe that it is only in an environment of choice between good and evil that the kingdom of God really shines.

To remove all choices except right living (as we define it) from our society is like only dealing with the symptoms of cancer while leaving the actual cancer to grow and fester. Sin is the cancer, and so I choose not to place my focus on dealing with the symptoms of the sin cancer, but in allowing grace to abound much more. Until we deal with the real issue, the sinful heart of man, all of our attempts to change society will fail. Do we save the homosexual by taking away all of his rights and sending him back to the closet where he or she will continue to do the same abominable things or do we expose him to the unconditional love of God and the power of the Gospel to bring deliverance? Do we reduce abortions in our country by making laws which will allow back alley butchers to thrive, or do we as a church create alternatives that give young ladies who have erred the hope to go on living?

I chose to vote for Obama because although there are areas in which we disagree, I believe that he will do what is best for the nation. For eight years we have been under a President who was touted by the so-called "Christian Right" as being a godly man, chosen by God to lead this nation in righteousness. Are we really better off now then we were eight years ago? At the time of this writing Mr. Bush is still the president and with that comes respects and honor and my prayers are with him and his family; however, I like to make known some of the issues under his leadership that created some unrest in this great country of ours.

The message he presented to us about weapons of mass destruction led us into a war with a country that had little or nothing to do with the attacks of 9/11. In some cases it appears that our soon-to-be former president has allowed his administration to run roughshod over the rule of law and respect for human rights. In 2004, our 43rd president won reelection by invoking the Christian community who were against abortion and homosexual marriages. I have asked some of my peers in ministry who voted for Mr. Bush for his second term against Senator John Kerry what substantive thing has he done to really reduce these issues?

These same Christian ministers understand that abortion and homosexuality are not the only sins that are referenced in the Bible. Many believe that leading an unjust war to seize control of oil, taking from the poor to make the rich richer, or detaining people indefinitely without charges and no legal representation is just much a sin as abortion and homosexuality.

It has been reported Mr. Bush has ridiculed the Christian evangelical base that elected him. McCain has also had a rocky relationship with the Christian world – only recreating himself in this election to get our vote. Sarah Palin appears by all accounts to be very sincere in her Christian faith; however just because one is a Christian does not qualify you to be Vice President of this vast secular nation. Unfortunately most fundamental Christians are confused on this issue and are taken advantage of by the unscrupulous politicians who use certain "Christian" tag words to win our vote and then forget about their promises until the next election.

I think that it is time for us Christians to wake up and realize that it is not the job of a free democratic society to usher in the kingdom of God. It is the job of our secular democratic republic to assure that everyone has the same rights and protections — whether we agree with their choices or not. For that reason, as a private citizen in this nation, I chose to support Barack Obama as the person who I thought would be the most equitable and fair in enforcing the rights of all.

It is however, the job of the church to present the kingdom of God in such power that people are transformed into citizens of that kingdom more than of any human government including the United States of America. For that reason, we must build that irresistible New Testament church that will once again turn our world upside down. This will happen not through an election, but through a revival!

The Curse that Never Was

"And Noah awoke from his wine, and knew what his younger
son had done unto him. And he said, Cursed be Canaan;
a servant of servants shall he be unto his brethren."
Genesis 9:24-25

Many black believers for years felt that this passage of scripture meant that the black race was cursed. Noah's three sons were Ham, Shem, and Japheth and of these three sons were the races established. Ham was the progenitor of the black race, Shem the Asian race, and Japheth the Caucasian race. Canaan, from the above-mentioned scripture, was the son of Ham.

Noah gave this pronouncement after awakening from a drunken stupor and realizing that he had been betrayed. In the Bible, it is referred to as "nakedness of the father". Now if the black race had been cursed by Noah to always serve the other races, wouldn't it make sense that Noah would have pronounced the curse on Ham? The curse was placed on Canaan and not Ham.

Let's take a look at what this man of God prophesied. He said, "Cursed be Canaan; a servant of servants shall he be unto his brethren." Genesis 9:25. What about Canaan? Whatever became of him? If you trace the lineage of Canaan, then you will find that they are the modern day Palestinians – not blacks!

In 2008 they are still without land and are actually a people from all of the Middle-eastern nations that are desperately trying to come under a structural leadership. Their roots unfortunately, are planted in terrorist acts and they have at their leadership level full demonic assistance.

One of the ways that you can tell that a nation or a people are being led by the devil or being led by God is by checking out the foundation or roots. Look at the extreme care that is placed on the lives of the headship and the near misses on their lives. I am only going to briefly speak about two – Fidel Castro and Yasser Arafat.

Fidel Castro of Cuba has stayed in power since the 1959 revolution and after numerous attempts on his life by Cuban rebels, the CIA, and members of his own administration. Castro recently handed over power to his seventy-six year old brother, Raul, in July of 2006.

Yasser Arafat is another character to examine. He was in a military helicopter that crashed in the Sahara Desert. Arafat was the only survivor of the crash. He walked out of the wreckage and crossed the Sahara Desert alone. It has been said that it is almost impossible for a human, let alone a man nearly sixty-five at the time, to accomplish such a feat. People still do not know how he was able to survive. He also has survived wars, political crises and several assassination attempts. Yasser Arafat finally died in November of 2004 at the age of seventy-five. His official cause of death remains unknown.

According to my research and my beliefs, Palestinians are the descendants of Canaan; however, it is important that we understand that the cross of Christ gives the potential for the remove of every curse. If you do not accept and receive the propitiation of the blood of Jesus, then you are destined to live under whatever curse genetically that you are predisposed.

I am not saying that a Canaanite or anyone of Palestinian descent cannot be saved because as I just stated, anyone can be saved because of the cross. I am saying, however, as a people if you are only following the natural lineage, then you are under a curse that has never been lifted. If a person under the curse receives Christ and confesses their deliverance, then they are free.

Ham did not do anything immoral or perverted towards his father. Ham did however go into the tent and saw what was going on and then proceeded to tell his other brothers about it. This incident did involve Canaan his son.

The Bible speaks the truth about this type of behavior with several scriptures detailing brothers raping sisters and everything else. It is safe to assume then that if Ham had violated his father in any way, then the scripture would have spoken of it.

Ham was not cursed, but his son Canaan was cursed. Why? What exactly did Ham witness? Canaan was caught sleeping with one of his father's wives. If one of the sons sleep with one of his father's wives, then that is known in ancient Hebrew as "nakedness of his father".

What should have been obvious to all was never truly made plain to black believers. The result of this myth led to generations of black believers being bound by an untruth. This passage was used to condone slavery. Combine this with New Testament scriptures from the Apostle Paul about servants being obedient to their masters, and what you have is a spiritual inferiority complex that locks in perfectly with the natural inferiority complex that was placed on blacks due to slavery and Jim Crow laws.

Because of the Jim Crow laws, the terrorism of the KKK, and the disastrous early efforts to integrate, many blacks resigned themselves to second class status. Those blacks who aspired to be more were determined to be "uppity", rebellious, or in the words of other blacks "better than".

I would say that it has only been within the past twenty-five to thirty years did we dare to begin to think outside this assumed curse. Christianity was introduced to African slaves during their enslavement, and most of these slave masters were considered to be devout men of God. These men ingrained in the minds of slaves, who were more accustomed to tribal-based ritualism, the story of Jesus and Adam and Eve, but also ingrained in their minds the curse of dark skin and the sin of disobedience. Although liberated from their natural oppression, many blacks carried that ingrained belief system of inferiority with them.

Now if God-fearing and Holy Spirit-filled blacks believe that they are somehow inferior, can you imagine how those who are "unchurched" must feel?

One only needs to look at the attitudes of men and women who seek to demean themselves and others by living up to stereotypes that have plagued the black race for years. Thugs, gangstas, and "hos" are images presented in videos and movies that are glorified. This imagery does nothing more than promote a lower level of intelligence that many in the white race believed for years.

In 1984, when "The Cosby Show" debut on NBC there was an outcry about a black father who was a doctor and a black mother who was a lawyer raising their five children in a nurturing and stable environment. This outcry did not come from white

America which readily embraced the new show, but came from the black community who felt that such a family did not depict "real" black families.

To believe such nonsense is to continue to believe in a curse that never was. The recent election of Senator Barack Obama to the presidency has now help to eradicate the belief.

When Obama first announced his intentions to run for president, many blacks viewed him as a lightweight non-contender. Many blacks still had fond memories of the Clintons. In 2006 at the funeral of Coretta Scott King, former President Bill Clinton received the loudest applause and overshadowed the likes of President Bush and other celebrities in attendance. His wife, Hillary, was viewed as the frontrunner for the Democratic nomination.

Obama was an Ivy-league educated young man with a beautiful wife who was also Ivy-league educated. They were intelligent, hard-working people with two beautiful daughters and a commitment to public service. Why was it so hard to believe that he could be president? *"A servant of servants shall he be unto his brethren"*. Did this supposed curse factor into the belief that there was no way a black man could ever be president?

When Obama won the Iowa caucuses, people began to take notice of this Senator with the funny name. I would hear statements such as, "You mean to tell me that the white people of Iowa actually voted for Obama?" It wasn't until the South Carolina primary however, did African Americans by the bus loads begin to get onboard and thus change the dynamics forever.

Now don't get me wrong. I am not saying that the Obamas were the first successful black family to change the mindset of African-Americans. That would be foolishness on my part. There are thousands of successful African American families throughout the United States. We have had our fair share of Congressmen, Senators, Supreme Court justices and Cabinet members.

We even had two men run for president with Jesse Jackson and Al Sharpton. These two men, however, were never considered serious contenders and because of their civil rights backgrounds would have had serious trouble with mainstream America. With Obama's victories in Iowa and South Carolina, we were now witnessing a black man as a frontrunner of for a major political party nomination. That was unheard of in America!

A black man had never even been seriously considered for the Vice President position, let alone for President! What shook things up even more was the fact that blacks had long been considered "in the pockets" of Hillary Clinton and after South Carolina, they left her almost overwhelmingly for Obama.

The perception of African Americans towards one of their own had shifted. It was almost as if the scales had fallen off our eyes and we were able to witness a new thing. As I mentioned before, we were accustomed to seeing successful African Americans like Colin Powell, Condoleeza Rice, and the late Thurgood Marshall, but this was different. For so long, it seemed as though the only people who were able to gain any type of status in our community were either sports stars or entertainers.

Obama became a phenomenon unlike anything ever seen in the black community while at the same time smashing stereotypes and perceptions in the rest of the United States as well. When I say that the reproach is lifted, this is exactly what I am talking about. In order for something to be lifted, there had to been some kind of judgment in place. In the next chapter, I am going to explore in depth the types of judgments that had shackled us for years and the glorious release that Obama's election brings.

The Entertainment Hoax

As I mentioned in my previous chapter, many blacks because of the ingrained belief of inferiority, never saw themselves as ever being "President of the United States". Instead many turned to what they knew was a surefire way to the top – athletics or entertainment. There was a time in our community that we believed that sports was the only path to success and respectability. This thinking was one of those reproaches that I have been speaking about. This type of thinking helped some blacks obtain a great living, but it is my belief that the blind pursuit of sports led to a decrease in the pursuit of academics. It was swallowing up thousands of talented young men who might otherwise have become lawyers or entrepreneurs. The odds of becoming a multi-millionaire athlete are slimmer than ever but that has not stopped families, friends, and other supporters of young black men of pursuing this dream.

Before the reproach was lifted, it was fact in so many of our communities that AIDS, crime, violence and drugs were sending increasingly numbers of young black men either to America's jails or the graveyards. With very few options, left for them sports became the hook that could pull them back from the bottomless pit. The athletic dream, no matter how unrealistic, offers at least a ray of hope to an increasingly hopeless generation. It was the only avenue where blacks could be the majority in something – the one thing in which blacks could establish businesses and their families could pass their wealth on to the next generation.

Throughout our history we have had some outstanding athletes who overcame enormous odds to succeed. Joe Louis, Jackie Robinson, Arthur Ashe, and Jim Brown are just some of the notables. These men were followed by Kareem Abdul Jabbar, O.J. Simpson, Walter Payton, Magic Johnson and Dr. J.

In the past twenty years, the hero worship of athletes exploded with Michael Jordan, Kobe Bryant, Michael Vick, Allen Iverson, Lebron James and Shaquille O'Neal. Instead of aspiring to be CEOs, engineers, or lawyers, most black youth were trying to be "like Mike".

It starts at an early age with boys and girls as young as seven and eight years-old playing in AAU tournaments all over the country. There are some magazines that rank basketball talents of children in the third grade!!! This is pure exploitation at its finest, but there is no outrage from our community. We buy into it wholeheartedly because of the mindset that we had developed.

Now don't get me wrong. I am not against athletics. My daughter is a first class runner and sprinter and Lord willing I hope that she is able to even compete in the Olympics. Where I differ from other parents, however, is that I don't view athletics as her only path to greatness. My daughter is also a top honor student who is on a path which I hope will lead her to Harvard. I am also not alone in this thinking. There have been many high profile athletes who were committed to educational excellence who were pushed by their parents to succeed academically.

It has only been within the past fifteen years that the academic bar has now been raised and black participation in collegiate sports is being restricted. It is now even impossible for youngsters to go straight from high school to the NBA. Stiffer NCAA admission requirements – without a concurrent improvement in high school academic preparation – are keeping more and more black athletes out of college. Schools and local governments are cutting youth sports programs to meet shrinking budgets. Inner city playgrounds and recreational centers are falling into disrepair and increasingly becoming the province of gangs and drugs dealers.

This can lead to a horrible cycle that young boys and girls find themselves. The idolization of athletes helped feed the perception that we as a race can only achieve due to our physical talents and not our minds. During slavery, our physical acumen was well known and because of this acumen we were able to build this great nation of ours. We however should aspire to be known for more than our physical presence, because there is also a downside to such physical superiority – FEAR!

That's right, FEAR! Throughout history we have seen what happens when one group of people fear another group of people because of some perceived superiority. Although Joseph as governor helped saved the Egyptians during their time of famine, the Bible states that there came a time when the Egyptians forgot all about Joseph and began to fear the increasing numbers of Israelites.

"Now there arose a new king over Egypt, which knew not Joseph. And he said unto his people, 'Behold, the people of the children of Israel are more and mightier than we. Come on, let us deal wisely with them; lest they multiply, and it come to pass, that when there falleth

out any war, they join also unto our enemies and fight against us, and so get them up out of our land."
Exodus 1:8-10.

Because of their numbers, the children of Israel inspired fear from the Egyptians. Black men because of their perceived physical presence throughout the years inspired fear from many whites. Think about it. What has been one of the most enduring images of our culture? It is of the raging, big black man who lacks control.

There have been many athletes who at the pinnacle of their fame inspired both whites and blacks alike, but when these same men "fell from grace" the reactions to their fall was visceral. One only needs to look at the cases of O.J. Simpson, Kobe Bryant and more recently, Michael Vick to understand this completely. Many felt that these men were only doing what comes natural to "their kind".

It is not my intent to debate the merits of their acts, but it is my intent to draw on the fact that these men should have never been put on a pedestal in the first place. Shine the spotlight on those individuals who are living a life that is a testament to all, taking care of their children, and serving their communities. Does this kind of individual sound familiar? It should. I am describing the 44th President of the United States – Barack Obama.

The entertainment industry is far worse than the sports industry. For years, we were always displayed as either servants or buffoons. Now to be a butler or a maid is not a dishonorable profession. What is dishonorable is to assume that is all we can aspire to be. There were some undoubtedly very talented actors whose only claim to fame came from unfortunately playing subservient roles. Why? Because that was the only thing that Hollywood would offer them.

Sidney Poitier, Lena Horne, Harry Belafonte, Billy Dee Williams, Diana Ross, Denzel Washington, Will Smith are all individuals who have commanded the big screen because of the work of those who came before them.

What is the excuse now for offering up images of buffoonery? Two reasons with the first being money and the second being a diminished mindset. I mentioned in an earlier chapter about the glorification of thugs, gangstas and buffoons. Unfortunately, the glorification of these images and songs have led to millions of dollars for the entertainment industry and can easily been seen in the music videos and reality television shows.

What has been the result? In addition to the sports idols, we now have a generation of young people being raised to be the next 50 Cent, Jay-Z, Lil Wayne and Flava Flav. When you see young black men sagging their pants down below their behinds or young ladies who feel that they can only be noticed by wearing low-riding pants with their thongs showing, it brings sharp pangs to the heart.

One of the most remarkable things about Barack Obama is that by being true to himself he has helped to change that perception of FEAR and FOOLISHNESS! I would like to point out something else as well. If you take a look at the individuals that surround Obama, you will also notice successful brothers who are lawyers, CEOs and businessman.

Obama represents a broad coalition of what can be and of what is. He is a president who enjoys playing basketball and who also has Jay-Z in his I-Pod, but he has never demeaned himself or played to stereotypes that would have sent mainstream America running for the exits. He didn't just stop at being the Senator from Illinois. He dared to dream bigger than the box that he had been placed. That message is one that should go to all ages zero to 99. If you have the God-given talent to succeed on the basketball court, football field, baseball diamond, or the race track, then go for it! If you can sing like an angel and can command the screen, then again I say shoot for the stars. Just know that now that we can be more because one man decided that he could be more. Dream to go higher.

Reconciliation of the Races – The New Man

What made Barack Obama stand out amongst all the other candidates who decided to run for president was his unique family history. Everyone should know by now the story of his origins. He is the son of a white woman from Kansas and an African man from Kenya who met while attending the University of Hawaii. The rest as they say is history.

Did Obama's mixed racial heritage factor into his winning the election? I would like to think so. Obama never shied away or tried to hide the fact that it was his white family members who raised him after his Kenyan father abandoned him and his mother. His story is eloquently told in his autobiography, *Dreams from my Father*.

Those who are closest to him, mention that Obama represents the best aspects of both of his parents. His mother was often viewed as idealistic where his father has been described as ambitious and serious. I believe that although he was very influenced by his white mother and his maternal grandparents, Obama probably did not know his true purpose until he visited Kenya and learned more about his father and his father's people. Obama is a true African-American in very sense of the word. His success was not only celebrated in the streets of the United States, but a joyous celebration occurred throughout Kenya as well.

I mentioned earlier that the three races can all be traced to the sons of Noah. Ham, the black race, Shem, the Asian race, and Japheth, the white race, all came from one man, Noah. God created us all and we were all created in his image. Although each race has its own defining characteristics, we are all still one in God's eyes.

When I watch what Obama has achieved, I cannot help but think about another prominent African-American of mixed heritage – Tiger Woods. I believe that Tiger Woods is the walking, living and breathing embodiment of the "reconciliation of the races". Tiger's outstanding golfing achievements are indeed the results of physical talent, hard work and practice, but if you dig just a little deeper this is what you will find. Tiger demonstrates the strength of his "Ham" side (his father) and the intense ability to focus and concentrate which comes from his "Shem" side (his mother). The result of these two very different races has formed one of the greatest golfing talents that this world has ever seen.

For so many years, children of mixed race were seen as cast-offs of society. They were not fully embraced by either race and often trapped in "no man's land". Terms such as half-breed, Oreos, and mutts were often used to described them. If there was every anything positive said, it would often be about having "good hair", "pretty skin" or "passing". One of the biggest dilemmas that was presented to children of mixed heritage was that of having to choose a race to which associate. History always dictated that if there was any drop of black blood, then that person was black. That assumption, however, denies the fact that there are indeed other races present. It was never God's will for the races to be divided nor used to define who we are.

If we were to take a closer examination of world history, we would find that every race was given a specific time and era to rule. Throughout history, various dynasties were considered the rulers of that particular time. You had the Roman Empire, Ming Dynasty, the Egyptian dynasties. All of these represent a time and place when a specific group of people excelled or dominated. This has been proven and support by the word of the Lord in Acts 17:26,

"And hath made of one blood all nations of men for to dwell on all the face of the earth, and hath determined the times before appointed, and the bounds of their habitation;

Noah's prophetic words over his sons have come to fruition. In Genesis 9:27, Noah proclaimed, "God shall enlarge Japheth, and he shall dwell in the tens of Shem; and Canaan shall be his servant." Japheth's descendants are the Caucasians which according to the prophecy would be enlarged by God, but will dwell in the tents of Shem.

The greatest explorer in history was of Japheth's lineage – Christopher Columbus. Columbus was an Italian who Hollywood would have you believe sailed the seas to pillage and steal jewels. Columbus was a passionate and religious man who believed he was on a mission to reach people that needed to hear the message of the cross. That was the reason he passionately appealed to King Ferdinand and Queen Isabella of Spain to finance his trip. It was a miracle that he even made it across the Atlantic.

If one ever gets to see the replica of the *Pinta* and the *Santa Maria* located on the East Coast, then they would see how miraculous it was to cross the Atlantic in those wooden boats without the aid of electronics or radar. Columbus and other European explorers were the fulfillment of the prophecy of Noah that stated "Japheth enlarge his territory".

We continue to live in the era of white dominance, and who was just elected to helm the world's last superpower? A man of mixed heritage – Barack Obama. WOW! He embodies the reconciliation of the races. I cannot help but laugh at the rich irony that this brings. There are powerful things at work here and we can not be blind to what is transpiring right before our eyes.

Allow me for a brief moment to bring into spiritual focus what is occurring in the natural. The reconciliation of the races had to occur in order for God's will on earth to take place. I firmly believe in my spirit that God's will does not involve color.

The Apostle Paul wrote something that I think is very important and there was a reason why he wrote this particular scripture. Paul had issues regarding his treatment as an outsider by the original eleven apostles where personally mentored and trained by Jesus. Paul stated in II Corinthians 5:16;

"Wherefore henceforth know we no man after the flesh: yea, though we have known Christ after the flesh, yet now henceforth know we him no more."

Paul, after all, was a persecutor of the church and became a convert after Jesus had ascended into heaven. This is why Paul's admonition to them and us was that we not know him after the flesh.

Paul stated that we are to know Christ and the power of his resurrection, and the fellowship of his sufferings, being made conformable unto his death. *Philippians 3:10* It does not matter what color Jesus Christ was although there are those who would like to make an issue about Jesus being Jewish. The Bible mentions however that Jesus was dark-skinned and some black people take comfort in that thought. All of that however, is irrelevant when your goals are to know him "after the flesh".

In order for God to become man he would have had to come forth from a lineage to become one of us, and that is what he did. Lineage, heritage and genealogy are so important to God that many chapters in the Bible detail implicitly the family origin. You can clearly see this with the word "begat" when you read the New Testament. As a matter of fact, two out of the four gospels go to great lengths to trace the genealogy of Jesus, both from his mother Mary's side to his father Joseph's side. They trace it in the opposite direction from Adam forward to Jesus, and from Jesus backward to Adam.

When you research the genealogy of Jesus in the Gospels, you will find that the statement of Jesus being a Jew is not entirely accurate. He was a Jew but more importantly, he represented the three branches of the sons of Noah. Jesus had definite lineage from Ham, definite ancestors from Shem, and Jesus was also represented of Japheth.

His representation of all three races is what the Apostle Paul meant when he wrote "in the flesh". Jesus became this one new man so that something was created in him.

"Having abolished in his flesh the enmity, even the law of the commandments contained in ordinances; for to make in himself of twain one new man, so making peace."
Ephesians 2:15

Understand we are talking about the blood and the cross, however the cross did not create new flesh, the cross destroyed whatever flesh he was. The cross was a destructive killing process. What then created the new man? When the Romans took him to the cross, they thought they were just taking a delusional Jewish man who thought he was the King of the Jews.

This man was a traitor to the Roman Empire and had to be killed thus removing any form of threat to Herod or Caesar. When they took Jesus to be crucified they did not realize that what they were doing was taking the representative of the lineage of Ham, Shem and Japheth. All three were a part of Jesus' DNA, so when Jesus was nailed to the cross, Ham, Shem, Japheth and all of their descendants were nailed to the cross as well.

What was nailed to the cross? Not just a singular race. When Jesus was nailed to the cross, the sins of Ham, Shem and Japheth were all nailed to the cross. He represented us all. He wasn't just some white man or Jewish man who died for a bunch of black people.

I say that because for years as part of the brainwashing that blacks were subjected to Christ was always depicted as a Caucasian. This depiction was created by artists for their European kings, and that was the only kind of Jesus that they knew to draw. Often times when people worship, they close their eyes and when they picture Jesus, they immediately picture what Michelangelo or Leonardo da Vinci pictured Jesus to look like. That however, was not Jesus but a European image of what they thought Jesus looked like. That is why we need to be wise like Paul who stated, "I don't want to know him after the flesh".

We all freely have the opportunity to go to a dimension in our relationship with Christ that surpasses what he was in the flesh.

To know him as the "one new man" What is the one new man? It was not the crucified Christ. It was the resurrected Christ who created a new race with him being the father of this new race! That is why the Bible calls him the last Adam.

There was a first Adam and Noah produced three sons from who we all came from after the flesh. There is however a last Adam who took all three fallen branches and lineage to the cross. God then raised up one new man who has given us all a new genetic imprint. We are now called a holy nation.

I am not asking anyone to ignore their national identity, rather I am asking that with this new presidency and dawn of a new era that you get in touch with the important part of you. We had nothing to do with our ancestry, we have everything to do with embracing the change that is about to take place in our country.

Jesus Christ helped build a nation that you can be born into by choice. We have transferred our citizenship. We have a glorious new heritage and we have a dual citizenship. Barack Obama's election and his message of hope and change can walk in step with our Lord and Savior's message if we allow ourselves to transcend.

Rolled Away – The Reason for Barack

In the book of Joshua, the fifth chapter deals with the warrior episodes. The Israelites had just crossed the Jordan in miraculous fashion. The priests stood in the middle, the water dams up, and the Israelites walked over a dry river bed like they did forty years ago when they crossed the Red Sea. What follows next is somewhat special to the senses. At least 40,000 full-grown, bearded and burly warriors participated in what must have been the largest mass surgical procedure in history -- 40,000 circumcisions!

Flint knives flashing, foreskins flying, blood spilling all over the ground - that must have been quite a sight to behold, and add to the background the sound of convalescent groans and moans. The most powerful thing however, was yet to come and it was the pronouncement that the Lord made: ***"Today I have rolled away the reproach of Egypt from you."*** This place was known as "Gilgal" which means "roll". To this day the area is still referred as "Gilbeath Haaraloth" meaning 'hill of foreskins.'

This was the rolling away tissue on the hill of foreskins. Nice. A whole generation of Israelites had not been circumcised when they wandered in the desert awaiting the passing of their disobedient predecessors. It is certainly highly symbolic therefore for this new generation, poised to claim the Promised Land, to renew the covenant in this way.

I am struck that God should interject with a reference to Egypt at this point. Another nuance of meaning is added to an already poignant moment – "I have rolled away the reproach of Egypt for you". Their circumcision was now tied to the crossing of the Jordan; conversely, a reenactment of the Red Sea crossing. This historical watershed powerfully signifies the days of slavery cast aside and a new life of freedom begins. African Americans, with the recent election of Barack Obama, have finally been cut into the fabric of this country.

Every Caucasian or descendent of Japheth needs to understand that although you did not invent or create the racial tension that your ancestors were guilty of; some form of repentance still needs to take place. In November 2008, shortly after Barack Obama was elected the 44th president of the United States, Bob Jones University, located in South Carolina, apologized for its racist policies which included a ban on interracial dating that wasn't lifted until 2000 and refusal to admit black students until 1971. I truly believe that there are many more that need to repent.

It was never God's intent for the races to be inclusive and to never integrate. One of God's original commandments was to be fruitful, and multiply and replenish the earth. There is a three-part commandment in his blessings: Be <u>fruitful</u>, full of fruitfulness, <u>multiply</u>, or have children and <u>fill</u> the earth, which was a requirement for migration. Why would God want them to migrate to different parts of the earth and fill the earth and not live in one community forever? The Lord wanted them to have the glory of the earth. The three sons of Noah – Ham, Shem, and Japheth had settled in the crescent of the Mediterranean leaving whole regions of the earth undiscovered.

When they had refuse to migrate, God was forced to do what they were not willing to do and that is when the dispersion of the Tower of Babel took place. Why would God do this? What is the harm of seclusion? The answer is simple: Deformity. God's blueprint for our lives is formed in our DNA. Our DNA is the Morse Code of the body. When you put long and short beads on a string, then you can build a message. DNA is a string that tells everything about us. When a child is conceived, the biological parents bring two matching genes that make up every attribute about you.

Why did God create two genes? Because if there is a genetic flaw in the female or the male, then there is another set there to overcome the flaw. If there is a genetic flaw in a family or in a community and intermarriage begins to take place within that same family or community, then there will be no different genetic traits to overcome those flaws. Flawed genes will reproduce more flawed genes. We can clearly see this with the pygmy tribes of Africa.

These isolated people were discovered in African and they all had a mild form of crippled feet. They were a small group who had intermarried and their genetic weaknesses became their dominant traits. God did not birth these people to be less than 59 inches in height with crippled feet. They isolated themselves and then began to propagate the weak genes.

This same thing can happen today if we never choose to go outside of our own community. The genetic weaknesses of diabetes, cancer or heart disease will become dominant in one community. God said that it is better for us physically to migrate and to split up. God has a purpose for everything.

Just as I speak in the natural, the same applies in the spiritual realm as well. It is equally dangerous for church people to inbreed as it is for a community of people to inbreed. Cults are born when a church stops growing and there is no fellowship with other believers. Because of the lack of new messages or different materials, blasphemous doctrines and heretic messages arise leading scores of people astray. How poignant that this past November 2008 marked the thirty year anniversary of the Jim Jones massacre in Jonestown.

We don't just need multi-culturism, we need multi-revelations. One philosopher said to a hammer, "Everything looks like a nail." Often times when God gives us a revelation, we hammer that until people cannot wait to hear something else, and that is why variety is good. It is good to have input from health perspectives and teaching. The Apostle Paul stated in Acts 17:26, "*And hath made of one blood all nations of men for to dwell on all the face of the earth, and hath determined the times before appointed, and the bounds of their habitation.*"

The first rule of humankind on the earth was by the descendants of Ham. The second rule by the descendents of Shem, which produced the Messiah, Jesus. The third rule was by Japheth.

Ham produced the first great cities, hunting, music, art, and dancing. Some of the greatest architecture in the world was produced during the early reign of Ham. The Semitic race rose during the time of King Solomon. Solomon was the richest man to ever live. The temple that he erected would cost around eight billion dollars in today's economy. This was a reign that had immense power, influence and wealth.

Finally, Japheth navigated the globe and new nations and new people ruled the earth. Japheth's lineage is still ruling the earth, but is now under the leadership of a mixture of Ham and Japheth. Barack Obama has the talent of both his father and the ability to navigate like his mother.

If we were to remove Japheth's entire lineage from the earth, then we would have to take away most of the control of wealth in the earth and the influences. Washington, D.C., is the most powerful city in the world that Japheth rules. One of the youngest presidents in the history of the United States will bring new shades to the canvas of white leaders who came before him. Senator Barack Obama has proved to be a biracial icon who can mobilize blacks and whites alike. I believe that it is his mixed lineage that gave him the background needed to create the dialogue that has bridged some of our divides.

God gave Ham his day, Shem his day, and Japheth his day to produce the glory of God in the earth and to seek after God and find him. God directed us to use the power, influence and wealth that he has given us to produce good in the earth. All three branches of mankind however were seduced by the power and the influence that gold and wealth can bring and they utterly failed.

It is my sincerest belief, that God has used Barack Obama in the natural so that we can come together in the spiritual and become the offspring of God. His election was representative of the symbol of God hearing all of the bloodshed of his people and the crying from the ground. Why else would someone like Oprah Winfrey, a billionaire and a media mogul, be crying on the shoulder of a man she had never met? When Barack and his family walked across that platform on November 4, 2008, it was a symbol of God hearing the cry of the black race. Our slavery is parallel to Israel: 400 years of slavery in Egypt. I am also reminded of the story of Rizpah, the mother of two sons who were slain because of Saul's disobedience. After their bodies were fastened to the wall for display, Rizpah settled in on the rock of Gibeah and remained there for five months to prevent them from being devoured by the beasts and birds of prey. Her cries were heard all the way to King David, who responded to her cries and had her sons buried as they should have been as king's children. Just as Israel's reproach had to be lifted before entering into their Promised Land, the reproach of the black race had to be lifted also. Now we can all see the importance of being the offspring of God.

The reproach has been lifted. African Americans no longer should have the mindset of always looking for a handout or "reparations". We should now be able to move beyond racism and not just tolerate, but now appreciate by understanding one another through education and assimilation. The racial divide in the United States is a fundamental divide but when you have other races in your own family it is hard to think of them as "other" anymore. We are seeing a blurring of the old lines and that has to be a good thing because the lines were artificial in the first place. We have the perfect example right before our eyes and we can now see it as Obama announces his Cabinet picks. He has chosen individuals from various backgrounds, ethnicities and talents.

The leader of our American family will be a shade darker than any one who has ever inhabited the White House. He will travel on Air Force One. His face will be placed on every government building and office. There will be magazine covers that will feature him and his beautiful family. Classroom history books will now be revised as we teach about Washington, Jefferson,

Lincoln, Roosevelt, Truman, Kennedy, Reagan, and Clinton. Barack Obama's name is now added to this list which is true assimilation.

Let me conclude by stating this. I do believe that it is very important to study your natural lineage. I believe that everyone should know about their ancestry. When you know your history, you are then able to appreciate what God has done for you. The recent election should help us all shake off the lies of the past and raise our heads up high.

It is my prayer that this book will create the answer to racial reconciliation and the strengthening of all communities in the United States and in the world. My utmost goal in writing this book was to help you identify yourself and then recognize that you are more than just a descendant of Ham, Shem and Japheth. You are the offspring of God, so now let us CELEBRATE!